THE
EUROPEAN
—= WORLD =—
400–1450

STUDENT STUDY GUIDE

OXFORD
UNIVERSITY PRESS

Oxford University Press, Inc., publishes works that
further Oxford University's objective of excellence
in research, scholarship, and education.

Oxford   New York
Auckland   Cape Town   Dar es Salaam   Hong Kong   Karachi
Kuala Lumpur   Madrid   Melbourne   Mexico City   Nairobi
New Delhi   Shanghai   Taipei   Toronto

With offices in
Argentina   Austria   Brazil   Chile   Czech Republic   France   Greece
Guatemala   Hungary   Italy   Japan   Poland   Portugal   Singapore
South Korea   Switzerland   Thailand   Turkey   Ukraine   Vietnam

Copyright © 2005 by Oxford University Press, Inc.

Published by Oxford University Press, Inc.
198 Madison Avenue, New York, NY 10016
www.oup.com

Oxford is a registered trademark of Oxford University Press

ISBN-13: 978-0-19-522258-6 (California edition)   ISBN-13: 978-0-19-522336-1

Editor and Project Director: Jacqueline A. Ball
Education Consultant: Diane L. Brooks, Ed.D.
Design: designlabnyc

Casper Grathwohl, Publisher

Printed in the United States of America
on acid-free paper

Dear Parents, Guardians, and Students:

This study guide has been created to increase student enjoyment and understanding of *The European World, 400–1450*. It has been developed to help students access the text. As they do so, they can learn history and the social sciences and improve reading, language arts, and study skills.

The study guide offers a wide variety of interactive exercises to support every chapter. Parents or other family members can participate in activities labeled "With a Parent or Partner." Adults can help in other ways, too. One important way is to encourage students to create and use a history journal as they work through the exercises in the guide. The journal can simply be an off-the-shelf notebook or three-ring binder used only for this purpose. Some students might like to customize their journals with markers, colored paper, drawings, or computer graphics. No matter what it looks like, a journal is a student's very own place to organize thoughts, practice writing, and make notes on important information. It will serve as a personal report of ongoing progress that your child's teacher can evaluate regularly. When completed, it will be a source of satisfaction and accomplishment for your child.

Sincerely,

Casper Grathwohl
Publisher

This book belongs to:

_____

CONTENTS

Chapter 1

Believers and Barbarians: The End of the Roman Empire

Rome felt pressure from internal conflicts and invasions by Germanic tribes. It split into two sections: the Western Roman Empire and the Eastern Roman Empire. At first Roman leaders brutally fought the spread of Christianity. Over time, Christianity became a dominant religion.

Chapter 2

Surrounded by "A Sea of Tribes": Europe Becomes Christian

Tribes such as the Franks, Visigoths, and Lombards took control of western Europe in early medieval times. Christianity spread throughout Europe from the 4th through the 7th centuries.

Chapter 3

Three Empires: Justinian, Charlemagne, and Muhammad

As ruler of the Byzantine Empire, Justinian rebuilt the city of Constantinople and created a unified code of laws. Charlemagne began a dynasty in Europe that turned the Frankish kingdom into an empire. Muhammad, founder of the religion of Islam, began an empire that unified an area stretching from Persia to Spain.

Chapter 4

A Good Knight's Work: War and Feudalism

During the 9th and 10th centuries, Vikings from Scandinavia raided European towns and cities. Under the system of feudalism, nobles formed relationships with knights to provide protection for their land. They also developed relationships with peasants to work their fields.

Chapter 5

Battle and Barter: From the Norman Conquest to the Rise of Trade

The Norman Conquest removed the Anglo-Saxons from power and brought the feudal system to medieval England. Germany saw the rise of religious influence and conflict between the power of the emperor and the pope. Peace and stability during the 12th century brought prosperity, the growth of towns and social classes, and a need to expand territories and settle new lands.

Chapter 6

Worlds in Collision: The *Reconquista* and the Crusades

Conflicts over territory broke out between Muslims and Christians in parts of Europe and Asia. Christian warriors drove out the Moors from their territories in Spain. The Islamic Seljuk Turks began conquering lands in Asia, threatening Constantinople. The pope urged nobles to recapture the Holy Land from the Turks, which began the First Crusade.

Chapter 7

Ladies, Lovers, and Lifestyles: The Flowering of Medieval Culture

The 11th and 12th centuries were a time of change in medieval Europe. Knights went from being warriors to being performers in mock battles. Nobility became interested in expressions of love and changed the ways that men behaved toward women. Even the ways that buildings were constructed changed. A strong woman, Eleanor of Aquitaine, was linked to many of these changes.

HOW TO USE THE STUDENT STUDY GUIDES TO
THE MEDIEVAL & EARLY MODERN WORLD

Each book in The Medieval & Early Modern World *introduces you to compelling adventures of fascinating men and women living at an amazing time. You will meet artists and warriors, rulers and scientists, merchants, traders, and slaves. You'll experience their lives close up, through diaries, letters, poems, songs, and myths.*

The events of the medieval and early modern time period changed the whole world forever. The foundations of international politics, the boundaries of countries, the roots of educational and religious institutions—all were established during this rich, electrifying period. We can't fully understand our world today without understanding how it connects with these times.

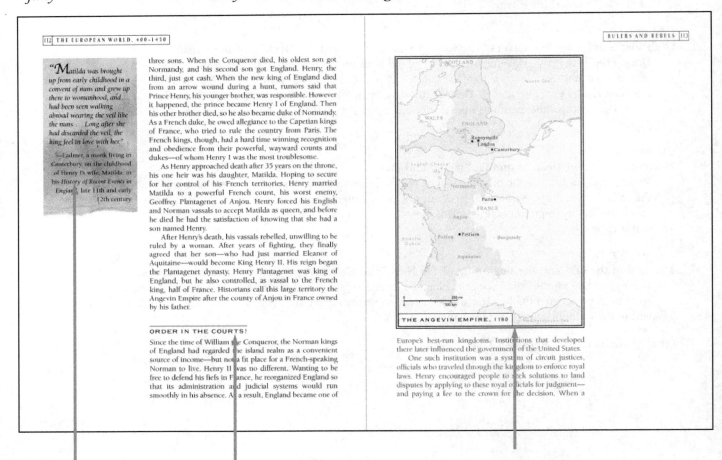

"*Matilda was brought up from early childhood in a convent of nuns and grew up there to womanhood, and had been seen walking abroad wearing the veil like the nuns. Long after she had discarded the veil, the king fell in love with her.*"

—Eadmer, a monk living in Canterbury, on the childhood of Henry I's wife, Matilda, in his *History of Recent Events in England*, late 11th and early 12th century

three sons. When the Conqueror died, his oldest son got Normandy, and his second son got England. Henry, the third, just got cash. When the new king of England died from an arrow wound during a hunt, rumors said that Prince Henry, his younger brother, was responsible. However it happened, the prince became Henry I of England. Then his other brother died, so he also became duke of Normandy. As a French duke, he owed allegiance to the Capetian kings of France, who tried to rule the country from Paris. The French kings, though, had a hard time winning recognition and obedience from their powerful, wayward counts and dukes—of whom Henry I was the most troublesome.

As Henry approached death after 35 years on the throne, his one heir was his daughter, Matilda. Hoping to secure for her control of his French territories, Henry married Matilda to a powerful French count, his worst enemy, Geoffrey Plantagenet of Anjou. Henry forced his English and Norman vassals to accept Matilda as queen, and before he died he had the satisfaction of knowing that she had a son named Henry.

After Henry's death, his vassals rebelled, unwilling to be ruled by a woman. After years of fighting, they finally agreed that her son—who had just married Eleanor of Aquitaine—would become King Henry II. His reign began the Plantagenet dynasty. Henry Plantagenet was king of England, but he also controlled, as vassal to the French king, half of France. Historians call this large territory the Angevin Empire after the county of Anjou in France owned by his father.

ORDER IN THE COURTS!

Since the time of William the Conqueror, the Norman kings of England had regarded the island realm as a convenient source of income—but not a fit place for a French-speaking Norman to live. Henry II was no different. Wanting to be free to defend his fiefs in France, he reorganized England so that its administration and judicial systems would run smoothly in his absence. As a result, England became one of

THE ANGEVIN EMPIRE, 1180

Europe's best-run kingdoms. Institutions that developed there later influenced the government of the United States.

One such institution was a system of circuit justices, officials who traveled through the kingdom to enforce royal laws. Henry encouraged people to seek solutions to land disputes by applying to these royal officials for judgment—and paying a fee to the crown for the decision. When a

Short quotes in sidebars tell about life in the words of someone living at the time.

Subheads give clues to the content to follow.

Geography has a lot to do with history. Maps show the locations of important places and supply a geographic context for important events.

This study guide will help you as you read the books in the series. It will help you learn and enjoy history while building thinking and writing skills. And it will help you pass important tests. The sample pages below show the books' special features. But before you begin reading the book or using this guide, be sure to have a notebook or extra paper and a pen handy to make a history journal. A dictionary and thesaurus will help you too. A special tip: Before you start a new chapter, read the two-part chapter title and predict what you will learn from the chapter. Check to see if you were right at the end.

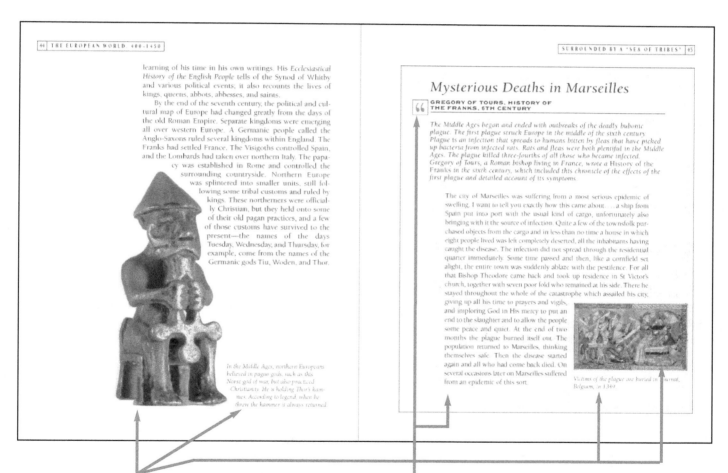

Pictures, often of artifacts, show important art and design of the times. Read the captions to learn even more than is in the text.

Every chapter has a long primary source quote that takes you back in time to the scene of an important action in a dramatic, powerful, first-person way. Look for these longer quotations marked by quotation marks followed by the source of the work.

On the next pages you will find models of graphic organizers. You will need these to do the activities for each chapter on the pages after that. Go back to the book as often as you need to.

GRAPHIC ORGANIZERS

As you read and study history, geography, and the social sciences, you'll start to collect a lot of information. Using a graphic organizer is one way to make information clearer and easier to understand. You can choose from different types of organizers, depending on the information.

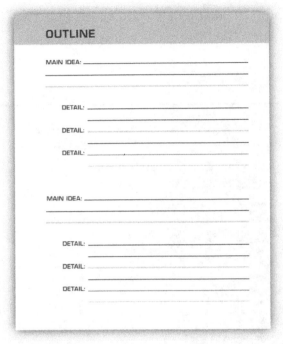

Outline

To build an outline, first identify your main idea. Write this at the top. Then, in the lines below, list the details that support the main idea. Keep adding main ideas and details as you need to.

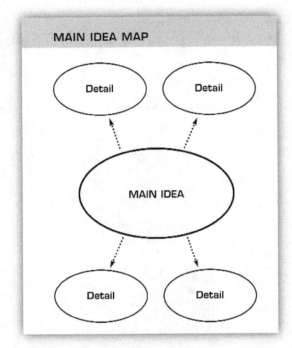

Main Idea Map

Write down your main idea in the central circle. Write details in the connecting circles.

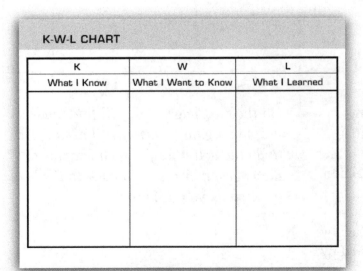

K-W-L Chart

Before you read a chapter, write down what you already know about a subject in the left column. Then write what you want to know in the center column. Then write what you learned in the last column. You can make a two-column version of this. Write what you know in the left and what you learned after reading the chapter.

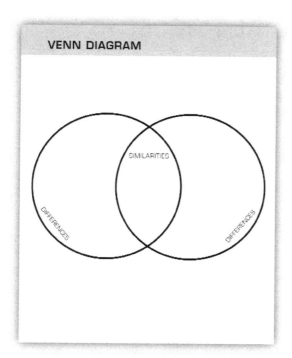

Venn Diagram

These overlapping circles show differences and similarities among topics. Each topic is shown as a circle. Any details the topics have in common go in the areas where those circles overlap. List the differences where the circles do not overlap.

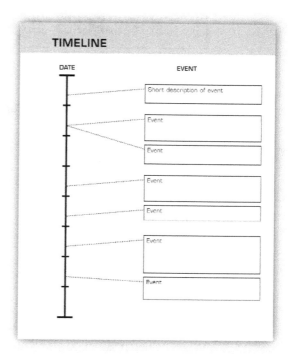

Timeline

A timeline divides a time period into equal chunks of time. Then it shows when events happened during that time. Decide how to divide up the timeline. Then write events in the boxes to the right when they happened. Connect them to the date line.

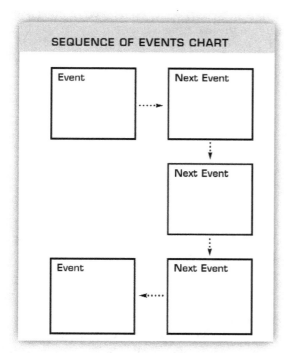

Sequence of Events Chart

Historical events bring about changes. These result in other events and changes. A sequence of events chart uses linked boxes to show how one event leads to another, and then another.

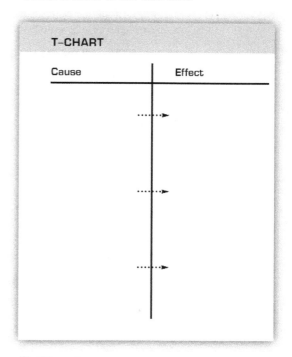

T–Chart

Use this chart to separate information into two columns. To separate causes and effects, list events, or causes, in one column. In the other column, list the change, or effect, each event brought about.

REPORTS AND SPECIAL PROJECTS

There's always more to find out about the European World during the Middle Ages. Take a look at the "Further Reading" section at the end of the book (pages 180–184). Here you'll find a number of books on different topics relating to medieval European history. Many of them will be available in your school or local public library.

GETTING STARTED

Explore the "Further Reading" section for any of these reasons.

— You're curious and want to learn more about a particular topic.

— You want to do a research report on medieval history.

— You still have questions about something covered in the book.

— You need more information for a special classroom project.

What's the best way to find the books that will help you the most?

LOOK AT THE SUBHEADS

The books are organized by topic. The subhead "Family Life" tells you where to find books about growing up in the Middle Ages. The subhead "Literature" recommends collections of tales and legends, poetry, and fascinating fiction and nonfiction. Go to "Biography" to locate life stories of Marco Polo, Joan of Arc, kings, queens, and conquerors. (Biographies of saints can also be found under "Religion.")

LOOK AT THE BOOK TITLES

The titles of the books can tell you a lot about what's inside. Under "Art and Architecture," you can tell at a glance which books are about cathedrals, which are about crafts such as tiling and masonry, and which are about art forms such as sculpture and illuminating.

LOOK FOR GENERAL REFERENCES

This section also lists general books, which are useful starting points for further research. "General Works on the Middle Ages" lists titles that provide a broad overview of the European World from 400 to 1450. Judge by the titles which books will be the most useful to you. Other references include:

— Dictionaries

— Encyclopedias

— Atlases

OTHER RESOURCES

Information comes in all kinds of formats. Use the book to learn about primary sources. Go to the library for videos, DVDs, and audio materials. And don't forget about the Internet!

AUDIO-VISUAL MATERIALS

Your school or local library can offer documentary videos and DVDs on the Middle Ages, as well as audio materials. If you have access to a computer, explore the sites listed in the section titled "Websites" (page 185) for some good jumping-off points. These are organized by topic, with brief descriptions of what you'll find on the site. Many websites list additional reading, as well as other Internet links you can visit.

What you've learned about the Middle Ages so far is just a beginning. Learning more is an ongoing adventure!

CHAPTER 1

BELIEVERS AND BARBARIANS: THE END OF THE ROMAN EMPIRE

CHAPTER SUMMARY

Rome felt pressure from internal conflicts and invasions by Germanic tribes. It split into two sections: the Western Roman Empire and the Eastern Roman Empire. At first Roman leaders brutally fought the spread of Christianity. Over time, Christianity became a dominant religion.

ACCESS

As you preview the chapter, skim and use illustrations, titles, and subheadings to jot down what you can infer about the fall of the Roman Empire and the spread of Christianity in the first column of the K-W-L chart. Write down what questions you have about these topics in the second column. As you read the chapter, look for answers to your questions. Write them in the third column of the chart. Some examples are listed below.

K	W	L
WHAT I KNOW	**WHAT I WANT TO KNOW**	**WHAT I LEARNED**
The Roman Empire fought against Germanic tribes. Early Christians were persecuted by Roman leaders. Constantine was a great leader. Augustine converted to Christianity	Why did the Roman Empire fall?	The Roman Empire fell because of internal conflicts and because of attacks by outsiders.

CAST OF CHARACTERS

On the lines provided below, write a few sentences about each person or group's relationship to the Roman Empire.

Augustine (aw-GUS-teen) _____

_____

Constantine the Great (Kon-stun-teen) _____

_____

Visigoths (VIH-zih-goths) _____

_____

WORD BANK

Choose five of the six words below and use them to write a paragraph about the Roman Empire in your history journal.

empire   citizen   Christianity   convert   barbarian   drought

WORD PLAY

Look up the word you didn't use in the dictionary. Find out its origin. Explain how the word's original meaning relates to its current meaning.

WITH A PARENT OR PARTNER

One of the forces of Germanic migration was a drought in the 4th century. With a parent or partner, research other famous or catastrophic droughts from another time period in history. Create and illustrate a chart that contrasts life in the area, community, or culture before and after the drought. Display your chart in the classroom.

CRITICAL THINKING
CONTRASTING CULTURES

The end of the Roman Empire was a turbulent era as the cultures of the Romans, the Christians, and the barbarians clashed. A **contrast** tells how two things are different. Words that signal contrasts include *however, on the other hand,* and *but.* Look at this example.

CONTRAST
The ancient Roman religion is based on the belief in many gods. Christianity, **however**, is based on the belief in one God.

Look at pages 28 and 29 in the Student Edition to find ways in which the Germanic tribes and the Roman/Mediterranean civilizations differed. Create categories for the kinds of differences, then list details for each culture. The first one is done as an example for you. Discuss your answers with a partner.

Category	Mediterranean/Roman cultures	Germanic cultures
Environment	Urban cities	Rural areas

WORKING WITH PRIMARY SOURCES

Read the law of the Franks, a Germanic people, reproduced here as well as on Student Edition page 29.

> If anyone has assaulted and plundered a free person, and it be proved upon him, he shall be [fined] 2,500 dinars, which make 63 shillings. If a Roman has plundered a Frank, the above law shall be observed. But if a Frank has plundered a Roman, he shall be [fined] 35 shillings."

IDENTIFYING POINT OF VIEW

The first Germanic kings copied the Roman practice of writing codes of law. In the late 400s, for example, King Euric, the Visigoth king of Gaul, wrote the Germanic customary law into code.

1. What crimes does the law address?

_____

_____

2. Why do you think customary laws, or laws based on tradition and custom, were eventually written down?

_____

_____

3. What does the law show about the Franks' attitudes toward the Romans at this time?

_____

_____

4. Do you know of any other laws in history that showed bias toward one group of people in a society? Give examples.

_____

_____

WRITE ABOUT IT

In your history journal, write an essay in which you invent a rule or law for your community, family, or school that you believe would improve the quality of life for everyone. Write about why the rule is important, how it would be enforced, and what would change as a result.

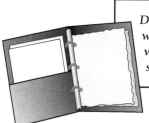

HISTORY JOURNAL

Don't forget to share your history journal with your classmates, and ask if you can see what their journals look like. You might be surprised—and get some new ideas.

ALL OVER THE MAP

Directions Follow the steps below to complete the map.

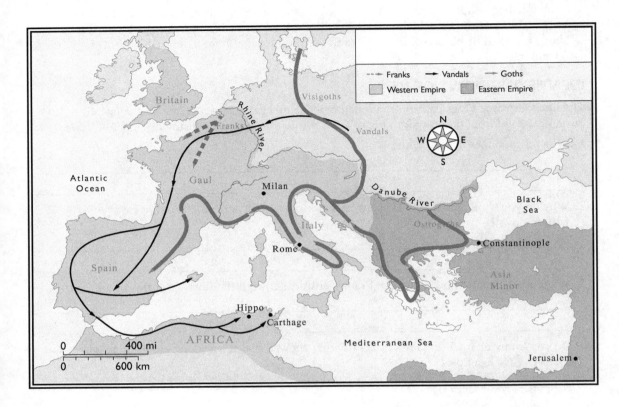

- Scan pages 28-32 of the Student Edition to find information on the migrations of the Franks, Vandals, Visigoths, and the Huns.
- Look at a physical-political map of modern Europe and Asia in an atlas.
- Write the mountain ranges on the map here.
- Label the Balkan Peninsula.
- Label Central Asia.
- Draw a line showing the approximate migration route of the Huns.
- Add the line representing the Huns and the term *Huns* to the legend.
- Write a paragraph in your history journal that answers these questions.
  - What were the natural boundaries of the Roman Empire's northern frontier?
  - What physical features affected the migrations of each group?
- Give your map a title that explains what the map shows.

SURROUNDED BY "A SEA OF TRIBES": EUROPE BECOMES CHRISTIAN

CHAPTER SUMMARY

Tribes such as the Franks, Visigoths, and Lombards took control of western Europe in early medieval times. Christianity spread throughout Europe from the 4th through the 7th centuries.

ACCESS

As you read Chapter 2, think about the reasons why things happened. These reasons are **causes**. Then think about what happened as a result of the causes. These are **effects**. To organize the information presented in the chapter, complete the chart below with the effects of each cause. The first one is done for you.

CAUSE	EFFECT
Rome could not stop barbarian invaders.	Visigoths, Franks, and Lombards took control of areas in France, Spain, and Italy.
Clovis, King of the Franks, became Christian.	
Romans and members of German tribes intermarried.	
Christian missionaries went to convert pagans in England, Ireland, and northern Europe.	
Monks copied manuscripts and kept libraries.	

CAST OF CHARACTERS

On the lines provided below, write a few sentences about why each character was important.

Sidonius Apollinaris (sigh-DOE-nee-us uh-Pall-uh-NAR-us) _____

_____

Clovis (KLOW-vus) _____

_____

Clotilda (Kluh-TIL-duh) _____

_____

Gregory of Tours (tour) _____

_____

Saint Patrick _____

_____

Benedict (BEN-uh-dikt) _____

_____

Bede (BEED) _____

WORD BANK

civic   pagan   unify   inheritance   infighting   culture   monastery

Choose words from the Word Bank to complete the sentences. One word is not used at all.

1. _____ was common among the Franks when a father divided land and possessions among his sons.

2. Monks lived at a _____ where they devoted their lives to prayer.

3. Bishops were both religious and _____ leaders during medieval times.

4. As Christianity spread, it helped to _____ the people of Europe.

5. Some tribes in northern Europe claimed to be Christian but continued some of their _____ practices from the past.

6. The _____ of Europe changes as Romans and Germanic tribes shared ideas and customs.

WORD PLAY

Look up the word that you did not use in the dictionary. Note the word's definition and part of speech. How does taking away its suffix (ending) change its part of speech? In the space provided below, write an original sentence using the word as both a noun and as a verb.

_____

CRITICAL THINKING
MAKING INFERENCES

Authors expect readers to use what they already know to understand new ideas. This is called **making inferences**. Look at the first sentence in Chapter 2. What inferences can you make, even if you don't know a lot about life in Rome?

The author wrote:	"Sidonius Apollinaris was a Roman man of high social status—so high that he married the emperor's daughter."
Ask yourself:	• Was "high social status" likely to be good or bad? • Is an emperor an important person? • Would marrying an emperor's daughter be good or bad?
Inferences you can make:	• High social status was important in Rome. • Only a man of high social status could marry an emperor's daughter. • Marrying the emperor's daughter was a good thing for Sidonius.

Read these ideas from Chapter 2 and answer the questions that follow.

1. Although Sidonius lived far from Rome, to him Rome remained the center of civilization. What inference can you make about what Sidonius thought of the place where he lived?

_____

2. Sidonius looked to Christianity to preserve learning and bring civilization to the barbarians. What inference can you make about what Sidonius thought of the barbarians?

_____

WORKING WITH PRIMARY SOURCES

Read Bishop Gregory of Tours's description of the cathedral in Clermont-Ferrand, which also appears on Student Edition page 39.

> The whole building is constructed in the shape of a cross. It has fifty-two windows, seventy columns and eight doorways. In it one is conscious of the fear of God and of a great brightness.

IDENTIFYING POINT OF VIEW

On the lines provided below, answer the following questions to analyze Gregory of Tours's point of view.

1. Think about the role of the man who described the cathedral. How might being a bishop have influenced what Gregory of Tours thought about a religious building?

   _____

   _____

2. Why might Gregory have included information about the numbers of windows, columns, and doorways in his description of the cathedral?

   _____

   _____

3. What might Gregory mean by "the fear of God"? Why might a cathedral give someone a fear of God?

   _____

   _____

4. Gregory describes "a great brightness" in the cathedral. The brightness could be the result of the many windows in the building. What symbolic or religious meaning might the phrase have?

   _____

   _____

5. How do you think a Visigoth leader would have described the cathedral? Why?

   _____

   _____

WITH A PARENT OR A PARTNER

Make a list of buildings or structures that have symbolic significance as well as perform a function. For example, the Great Wall of China was a defensive barrier, but its impressive size also symbolized the greatness of the ancient Chinese dynasties. Your list could include government buildings, churches, museums, theaters, sports facilities, bridges, or dams. Once you have brainstormed a list of symbolic structures, choose one and research its design and history. Create an illustrated poster to display your findings.

WRITE ABOUT IT

Think of a place that has personal and symbolic significance to you. You may associate this place with a certain feeling or emotion, such as peace, awe, comfort, or joy. It could be a public building—like a museum—or it could be a private place that few people visit—like your grandmother's attic. Write an essay in your history journal that uses descriptive imagery to "show" the reader your special place. Conclude your essay be explaining how visiting this place affects you emotionally.

ALL OVER THE MAP
LOCATION

Directions Use the information in the Student Edition to locate on the map the places where the following people lived or worked.

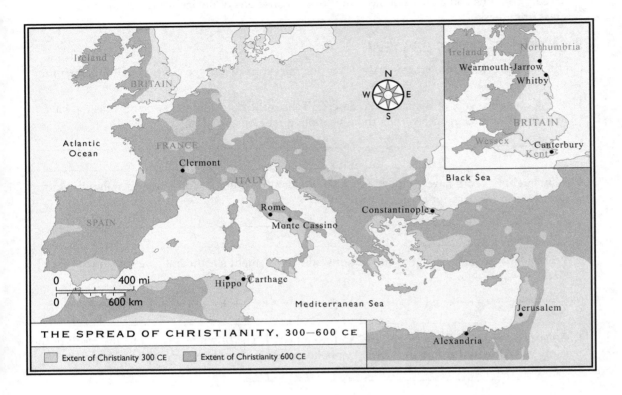

THE SPREAD OF CHRISTIANITY, 300—600 CE

Extent of Christianity 300 CE   Extent of Christianity 600 CE

- Scan the chapter for each name or group listed below.
- On the lines provided below, write the name of the area or specific place where each lived or worked.
- If no city or town is mentioned, write the name of the region or country where the person lived.
- On the map write the number for each name in the appropriate place to show where each lived or worked (thus creating a legend for the map that indicates the physical location associated with each historical figure).

1. Sidonius Apollinaris _____

2. Clovis _____

3. Clotilda _____

4. Gregory of Tours _____

5. Saint Patrick _____

6. Benedict _____

7. Venerable Bede _____

8. Benedictine missionaries _____

9. Irish missionaries _____

THREE EMPIRES: JUSTINIAN, CHARLEMAGNE, AND MUHAMMAD

CHAPTER SUMMARY

As ruler of the Byzantine Empire, Justinian rebuilt the city of Constantinople and created a unified code of laws. Charlemagne began a dynasty in Europe that turned the Frankish kingdom into an empire. Muhammad, founder of the religion of Islam, began an empire that unified an area stretching from Persia to Spain.

ACCESS

In Chapter 3 you will read about rulers and their empires. Use the chart below to organize and keep track of the information you read about each empire. Fill in the categories as you read.

	Byzantine Empire	Frankish Empire	Islamic Empire
Ruler	Justinian	Charlemagne	Muhammad
Area or Region			
Important Cities			
Achievements			
Problems or Mistakes			

CAST OF CHARACTERS

On the lines provided below, write two adjectives that describe each character and explain why you chose them.

Justinian (juh-STIN-ee-un) _____

Theodora (theo-DOOR-uh) _____

Charlemagne (SHAR-luh-mane) _____

Muhammad (mo-HA-mud) _____

WHAT HAPPENED WHEN

On the lines below, describe why each date was important.

527–565 _____

630 _____

Christmas Day 800 _____

WORD BANK

decree estate nobility peasant tenant revelation prophet

Choose words from the Word Bank to complete the sentences. One word is not used at all.

1. Muhammad said that he received a _____ from God that told him to found Islam.

2. The dukes and marquises appointed by Charlemagne were part of European _____.

3. As emperor, Justinian could give any order, or _____.

4. _____ did all of the work on a noble's _____.

5. Followers of Islam believe that Muhammad was a _____.

WORD PLAY

Look up the word that you did not use in the dictionary. Write a sentence using that word in a contemporary context.

_____

CRITICAL THINKING

FACT AND OPINION

A **fact** is a statement that can be proven. This means that there is a way to find out if the statement is true. An **opinion** is what someone thinks or believes. An opinion cannot be proved or disproved, like the example below.

	Can it be proven? How?	Fact or Opinion?
Justinian tried to conquer territory in the West that had once been part of the Roman Empire.	Yes. Check history books or encyclopedias.	fact

Decide whether each statement is a fact or an opinion, and explain how you know.

	Fact or Opinion?	How do you know?
1. Charlemagne used the threat of force to spread Christianity.		
2. Charlemagne appointed rulers to govern the regions he conquered.		
3. Eclipses were omens that predicted the end of Charlemagne's life.		
4. The Quran is a book that contains the teachings of Muhammad.		
5. Shiite Muslims believe that only the descendants of Muhammad should rule.		

WORKING WITH PRIMARY SOURCES

The following passage comes from Einhard's biography of Charlemagne. Read the passage and answer the questions.

> [Charlemagne] had the gift of ready and fluent speech, and could express whatever he had to say with the utmost clearness. He was not satisfied with command of his native language merely, but gave attention to the study of foreign ones, and in particular was such a master of Latin that he could speak it as well as his native tongue; but he could understand Greek better than he could speak it. He was so eloquent, indeed, that he might have passed for a teacher of eloquence.

DRAWING CONCLUSIONS

1. Why would the ability to "express whatever he had to say with the utmost clearness" have been important for a leader such as Charlemagne?

_____

_____

2. What advantage might Charlemagne's speaking ability have given him?

_____

_____

3. Based on what you have read about Charlemagne, why might he have wanted to speak more than one language?

_____

_____

4. If Charlemagne lived in modern times, what language or languages do you think he would learn to speak? Explain your answer.

_____

_____

5. Underline a sentence in the passage that is Einhard's opinion. Explain why the sentence you chose is an opinion.

_____

_____

WRITE ABOUT IT

Charlemagne had many skills that made him a strong leader, including his speaking abilities. What do you think is the most important skill or quality that a strong leader should have? Why? Write an essay in your history journal to explain and support your opinion.

HISTORY JOURNAL

Don't forget to share your history journal with your classmates, and ask if you can see what their journals look like. You might be surprised—and get some new ideas.

ALL OVER THE MAP
USING LATITUDE AND LONGITUDE

Mapmakers use a grid pattern to locate places on a map. Lines of latitude run east and west. Lines of longitude run north and south. To find a place's latitude and longitude, look for the place where the lines meet. For example, Constantinople is located at 41°N and 30°E.

Directions On the line after each set of latitude and longitude numbers, write the name of the city that is located there.

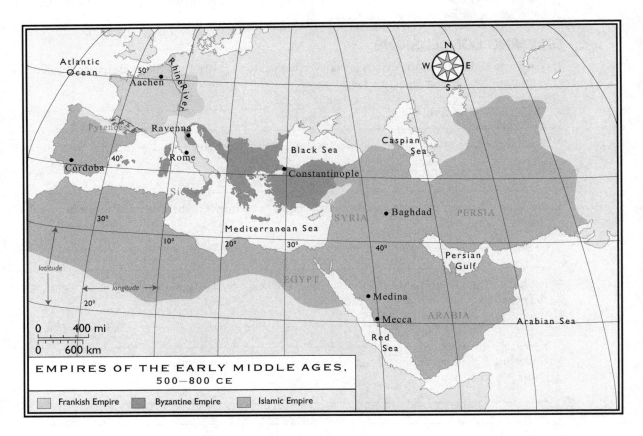

1. 42°N latitude and 12°E longitude _____

2. 44°N latitude and 12°E longitude _____

3. 33°N latitude and 44°E longitude _____

4. 24°N latitude and 38°E longitude _____

5. 21°N latitude and 40°E longitude _____

6. 50°N latitude and 6°E longitude _____

7. Where would you be if you were in the following location?

   43°N latitude and 32°E longitude? _____

8. Using an atlas, find the latitude and longitude for your own city or town.

A GOOD KNIGHT'S WORK: WAR AND FEUDALISM

CHAPTER SUMMARY

During the 9th and 10th centuries, Vikings from Scandinavia raided European towns and cities. Under the system of feudalism, nobles formed relationships with knights to provide protection for their land. They also developed relationships with peasants to work their fields.

ACCESS

Chapter 4 describes Viking raids, the relationship between knights and lords, the development of feudalism, and the lives of peasants. As you read the chapter, review the main ideas shown in the outline below. Complete the outline by adding details that support each main idea.

OUTLINE

MAIN IDEA: Vikings from Scandinavia went on raids throughout Europe.

DETAIL: _____

DETAIL: _____

DETAIL: _____

MAIN IDEA: Europe fought back against the Vikings.

DETAIL: _____

DETAIL: _____

DETAIL: _____

MAIN IDEA: Feudalism developed in Europe.

DETAIL: _____

DETAIL: _____

DETAIL: _____

MAIN IDEA: Peasant life changed by the 12th century.

DETAIL: _____

DETAIL: _____

DETAIL: _____

CAST OF CHARACTERS

On the lines provided below, write a paragraph that describes the long-term influences of the Viking invasions on Alfred, King of Wessex, and Hugh Capet (ka-PAY), King of France.

_____

_____

_____

_____

_____

_____

_____

WORD BANK

heir siege knight feudalism manor serf

Choose words from the Word Bank to complete the sentences. One word is not used.

In the system of _____, the lords had a lot of power over others. The lord controlled the land that was part of his _____. Each _____ was required to work the land. Each _____ pledged loyalty to the lord and fought for him. When a vassal died, the lord could impose a tax for passing the land to the vassal's _____.

WORD PLAY

Look up the word that you did not use in the dictionary. Write one sentence using the word in a historical context.

_____

WITH A PARENT OR PARTNER

The words *knight* and *night* are homophones. They sound the same but they have different meanings and spellings. Work with a parent or partner to list three other vocabulary words from this chapter that also have homophones. In your history journal, write humorous sentences using each pair of homophones. For example, *One night the knight tripped over his lance.*

CRITICAL THINKING
CAUSE AND EFFECT

The reason that something happens is called a **cause**. The thing that happens is known as the **effect**. Historical writers often use signal words such as *because, so,* or *as a result* to signal a cause-and-effect relationship. Discuss how changes in agriculture affected the lives of peasants.

CAUSE	EFFECT
New plows had blades to cut heavy sod.	**As a result,** previously unfarmed lands could be cultivated.

Think about events described in Chapter 4 that caused other events to occur. Write a cause or an effect in each space in the chart below.

CAUSE	EFFECT
1. Vikings had little agricultural land and a growing population.	AS A RESULT
2. The kings of France could not protect their people from the Vikings.	AS A RESULT
3.	AS A RESULT Only wealthy people became knights.
4.	AS A RESULT The vassals promised to fight for their lord.
5. Noblewomen had to run the estates while their husbands and fathers were fighting.	AS A RESULT
6.	AS A RESULT Few peasants moved from where they lived.

WORKING WITH PRIMARY SOURCES

Read an Irish monk's description of Viking raids from Student Edition page 61.

[A] hundred hard-steeled iron heads on one neck, and a hundred sharp, ready, cool, never rusting, brazen tongues in each head, and a hundred garrulous, loud, unceasing voices from each tongue . . . could not recount . . . what all . . . suffered . . . of hardship, of injury, and of oppression, in every house, from these valiant, wrathful, foreign, purely pagan people.

IDENTIFYING POINT OF VIEW

Because many monasteries were wealthy estates, they attracted the attention of Viking raiders. Monasteries were the centers of learning. When the Vikings plundered the monasteries, they destroyed great amounts of knowledge, too.

1. In the last line of the quote, how does the monk describe the Vikings? (*Use a dictionary to define any unfamiliar words.*)

_____

_____

2. What do you think the monk means by *oppression*? Check a dictionary if you are not sure.

_____

_____

3. How do you think the monk feels about pagans?

_____

_____

4. Study the image of the cross and its caption on page 72. Based on this illustration, how can you tell that the relationship between the Christians and the Viking invaders changed over time?

_____

_____

WRITE ABOUT IT

If you were making a movie about the Viking invasions of Europe, how would you portray the Vikings? Write a descriptive essay in your history journal that explains the following aspects of your film: the costumes you would design, the actors you would cast, and the directions you would give the actors. Conclude your essay by explaining whether your portrayal of the Vikings could be considered "historically accurate" and on what basis you made your decisions.

HISTORY JOURNAL

Don't forget to share your history journal with your classmates, and ask if you can see what their journals look like. You might be surprised—and get some new ideas.

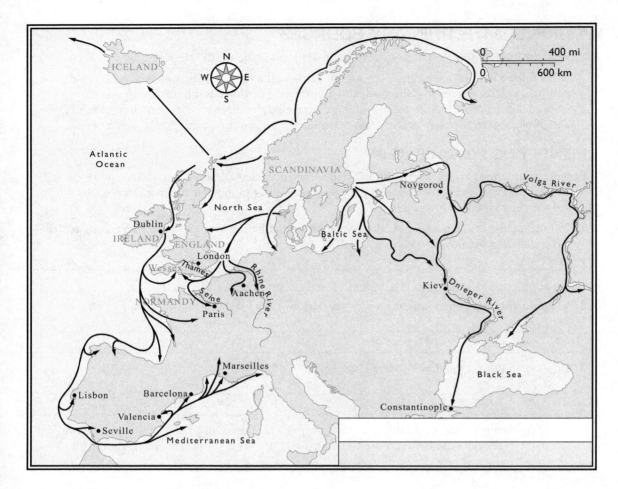

ALL OVER THE MAP

Directions Follow the steps below to complete the map.

- Scan pages 60–63 to find information on the Viking invasions.
- Make a list of key dates and events. Note where they took place.
- Make a small drawing, or icon, for each event. You might draw a small flame, for example, to represent an important raid.
- Draw each icon on the map in the appropriate location for that event, along with the date of the event.
- Make a legend for your map showing what each icon stands for.
- Give your map a title that explains what the map shows.

BATTLE AND BARTER: FROM THE NORMAN CONQUEST TO THE RISE OF TRADE

CHAPTER SUMMARY

The Norman Conquest removed the Anglo-Saxons from power and brought the feudal system to medieval England. Germany saw the rise of religious influence and conflict between the power of the emperor and the pope. Peace and stability during the 12th century brought prosperity, the growth of towns and social classes, and a need to expand territories and settle new lands.

ACCESS

In Chapter 5, events lead to other events in different parts of Europe. As you read about the Norman Conquest, complete the sequence of events organizer below to show how one event leads to another.

SEQUENCE OF EVENTS CHART

| Event: King Edward dies in 1066. He has no children, and no heir. Three men want to succeed him: the Anglo-Saxon nobleman Harold Godwinson, King Harald Hardrada of Norway, and Duke William of Normandy. | → | Next Event: |

| Next Event: |

| Event: | ← | Next Event: |

CAST OF CHARACTERS

On the lines provided below, explain why each character was important.

Harold Godwinson (GOD-win-sun) _____

Harald Hardrada (HAR-uld HARD-ra-duh) _____

William _____

Hildebrand (HIL-du-brant) _____

WORD BANK

salvation artisan depose conquest absolve reform

Choose words from the Word Bank to complete the sentences. One word is not used at all.

1. To help prepare for his _____ of England, William's fleet brought along supplies, warhorses, and materials for building castles.

2. In order to _____ the office of the pope, the German emperor appointed better-educated men.

3. Wealthy patrons contributed to the church in order to ensure their _____.

4. The nobles threatened to _____ Henry IV if he did not make peace with Gregory.

5. A skilled _____ would be in great demand among merchants looking for goods to trade in 12th-century European towns.

WORD PLAY

Write a sentence about one of the people from the Cast of Characters for this chapter that uses the word left over in the Word Bank.

_____

_____

CRITICAL THINKING
IDENTIFYING POINT OF VIEW

Just as it is helpful to identify a writer's point of view so that you can understand his or her arguments, identifying the points of view of historical figures can help you better understand historical events.

Think about how certain figures or groups of people discussed in Chapter 5 felt about other people or events. Write the letter of the point of view in the right column that matches the person or people in the left column.

PEOPLE	POINT OF VIEW
_____ 1. Pope Gregory VII	a. He believed he should succeed Edward because his Danish ancestor had once ruled England.
_____ 2. Harald Hardrada	b. In his view, the emperor sinned by performing the sacred rite of investiture.
_____ 3. Duke William of Normandy	c. They hoped to increase their power by enticing people to migrate to their towns.
_____ 4. lords of European towns	d. As brother to Edward's wife, he felt entitled to claim Edward's throne.
_____ 5. Harold Godwinson	e. Their skills allowed them to prosper and enjoy being in demand.
_____ 6. Emperor Henry IV	f. He called the pope a "false monk" because the pope had not been properly elected or appointed.
_____ 7. artisans in European towns	g. He claimed that Edward had promised him the throne.

WORKING WITH PRIMARY SOURCES

Examine the four-panel illustration of Pope Gregory VII and Henry IV on Student Edition page 81. In the top left panel, the pope excommunicates Henry. In the top right panel, Henry overpowers Gregory and brings in a new pope. In the bottom left panel, Gregory again excommunicates Henry; in the bottom right panel, Gregory dies. Their struggles were part of the great battle over who should have more power, the pope or the king.

IDENTIFYING MAIN IDEA AND DETAILS

The illustration shows events in the conflict between Pope Gregory VII and Henry IV. Answer the questions below to describe how the illustration tells about a main idea and how details in the illustration give the viewer additional information.

1. What main idea does the illustration show?

   _____

   _____

2. Look at the upper left section. What details identify each character? How do you know Gregory is more powerful here?

   _____

   _____

3. Look at the upper right section. What details help explain that Henry has won a battle?

   _____

   _____

4. Look at the lower left section. How can you tell that Gregory is more powerful here?

   _____

   _____

5. Look at the lower right section. What details help tell what has happened?

   _____

   _____

   _____

WRITE ABOUT IT

Tell a dramatic story from your own life in four illustrated panels, the way the conflict between Pope Gregory VII and Henry IV is told in the picture above and on page 81 of your Student Edition. Draw a sketch in your history journal in which you capture the most important characters and details, yet make the drawing simple enough that a viewer can understand it without a great deal of background information. Exchange history journals with a classmate and look at each other's drawings, then write a short narrative below it in which you describe what you think your partner's drawing depicts and why.

ALL OVER THE MAP

Directions Follow the steps below to complete the map.

- Review pages 71–73 to find information on the Norman Conquest.

- Mark and label the following places: England, Normandy, Norway, London.

- Mark and label the following geographic features: the North Sea, the English Channel, the Thames River.

- Choose colors to identify the three contenders to the English throne: Harold Godwinson, Harald Hardrada, and Duke William. Make a legend to explain who each color stands for.

- Use Harald Hardrada's color to trace a possible route he might have taken to arrive at England.

- Mark and label two places where major battles took place. Use your corresponding colors to indicate who battled in each place. Circle the victors' colors.

- Use Duke William's color to trace a route he might have taken to arrive in England. Then trace the route he might have taken to prepare to conquer London.

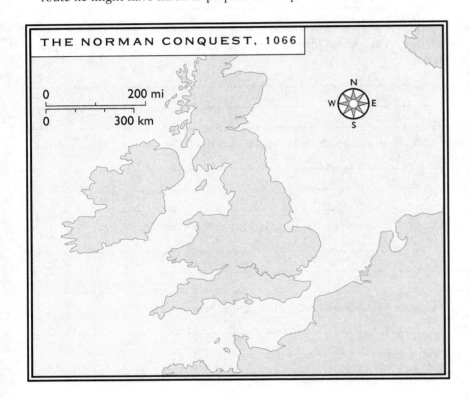

THE NORMAN CONQUEST, 1066

0 — 200 mi
0 — 300 km

GROUP TOGETHER

Wouldn't it be fun to know what other students think about the Norman Conquest? Was it a positive development for England in the long run? Get a few friends together and ask your teacher to help you organize a discussion group at school. Have one person take notes and another person present the group's ideas to the class.

WORLDS IN COLLISION: THE *RECONQUISTA* AND THE CRUSADES

CHAPTER SUMMARY

Conflicts over territory broke out between Muslims and Christians in parts of Europe and Asia. Christian warriors drove out the Moors from their territories in Spain. The Islamic Seljuk Turks began conquering lands in Asia, threatening Constantinople. The pope urged nobles to recapture the Holy Land from the Turks, which began the First Crusade.

ACCESS

Chapter 6 describes the sequence of events related to the *Reconquista* and the First Crusade. To organize the information in the chapter, use the timeline graphic organizer on page 9 of this study guide. As you read the chapter, look for dates and other sequence clues. Record the main events in the timeline below.

DATE

1072

EVENT

The de Hauteville brothers founded a Norman kingdom in southern Italy and on Sicily.
Event
Event
Event
Event
Event
Event

CAST OF CHARACTERS

On the lines provided below, explain why each character or group was important.

Rodrigo Díaz (rod-REE-go DEE-as) _____

Seljuk Turks _____

Urban II _____

Bohemund (BO-uh-mund) _____

WORD BANK

pilgrimage mercenary crusader epic Crusades pogrom relic

Choose words from the Word Bank to complete the sentences. One word is not used at all. Go back to the book to check information.

1. The nobleman hired the _____ to fight for him.

2. The Christians made a _____ to Jerusalem to visit holy sites.

3. *El Cid* is an _____ about the *Reconquista*.

4. Members of the popular army killed many Jews during the first _____.

5. The _____ believed he was fighting for Christianity.

6. The pope supported the battles against the Muslims, called the _____.

WORD PLAY

Look up the word that you did not use in the dictionary. Write a sentence using the word in a modern or contemporary context.

WITH A PARENT OR PARTNER

Make a timeline of your own life. Start with the year you were born and finish with the present date. Mark off and label years one by one. Write important events in your life when they happened. Then make a parallel timeline that corresponds to the same time period as your life. Include significant events in your community, state, the nation, or the world. Share and compare your parallel timelines with a partner at school.

CRITICAL THINKING
DRAWING CONCLUSIONS

A **conclusion** is a carefully thought-out understanding about an event or an issue. To draw a conclusion, you can combine **what you read** with **what you already know** about the topic. Look at the example below.

What I Read	What I Know	Conclusion
• The crusaders' conquest was bloody. • Christians and Muslims lived together, traded, and shared customs.	• Former enemies can coexist if it can benefit them. • Neighboring cultures often influence each other.	• After the First Crusade, Christians and Muslims in the Holy Land found it more beneficial to cooperate than to fight.

Read this paragraph from page 96 of the chapter. Use the information and what you know to draw a conclusion. Write your responses on the lines provided below.

What, the noble leaders of the crusade wondered, should they do with Jerusalem? The petty fighting and land-hunger that had marked their earlier conquests seemed inappropriate in the holy city itself. In the end, they named the only nobleman who had come on the crusade for genuine religious reasons as the first king of Jerusalem.

What I Read: _____

_____

What I Know: _____

_____

My Conclusion: _____

_____

WORKING WITH PRIMARY SOURCES

Read Emperor Alexius's daughter's description of Bohemund, from Student Edition page 94.

> There were among the Latins such men as Bohemund and his fellow counselors, who, eager to obtain the Roman Empire for themselves, had been looking with avarice [greed] upon it for a long time.

IDENTIFYING POINT OF VIEW

Emperor Alexius had conflicts with the main army of crusaders in Constantinople. He did not trust them. In fact, they broke their promise to him after he offered them aid. Use this information and what you already know to help you answer the following questions on the lines provided below.

1. How was the Roman Empire divided at this time in history?

_____

_____

2. Compare the daughter's opinion of the crusaders with that of her father, Emperor Alexius. How are they similar?

_____

_____

3. Based on what you read in the chapter, do you agree that the noblemen were greedy? Explain.

_____

_____

4. If you were Emperor Alexius, would you have offered aid to the noblemen? Why or why not?

_____

_____

WRITE ABOUT IT

The crusaders probably believed that they had valid reasons for breaking their promise to the emperor. Do you think it is ever right to break a promise? Write an essay in your history journal to explain and support your opinion. Make sure that you use concrete examples to support your stance. For example, you might want to describe a personal anecdote (short story) or a public event that demonstrates the importance of keeping a promise. Or you could explain actual circumstances where you felt the breaking of a promise was necessary or justified.

HISTORY JOURNAL

Don't forget to share your history journal with your classmates, and ask if you can see what their journals look like. You might be surprised—and get some new ideas.

ALL OVER THE MAP

Directions: Follow the steps below to complete the map.

- Scan pages 90–96 to find information on the events leading up to and during the First Crusade.
- Make a list of key dates and events. Note where they took place.
- Use a modern map of the region to find place names mentioned in the text.
- Make a small drawing, or icon, for each event. You might draw a small flame, for example, to designate a siege or a battle. You might draw a new line to show the popular army's route.
- Draw each icon on the map below to indicate the location of the event, along with the date of the event.
- Make a legend for your map showing what each icon stands for.
- Give your map a title that explains what the map shows.

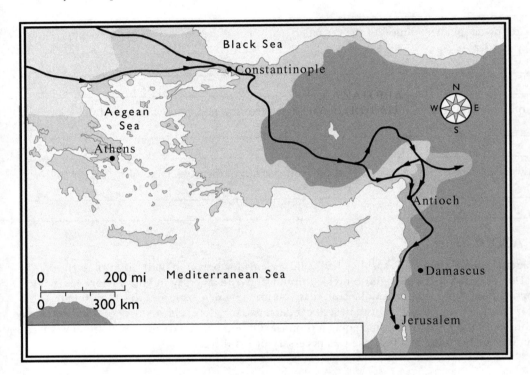

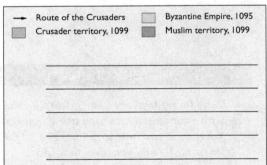

CHAPTER 7

LADIES, LOVERS, AND LIFESTYLES: THE FLOWERING OF MEDIEVAL CULTURE

CHAPTER SUMMARY

The 11th and 12th centuries were a time of change in medieval Europe. Knights went from being warriors to being performers in mock battles. Nobility became interested in expressions of love and changed the ways that men behaved toward women. Even the ways that buildings were constructed changed. A strong woman, Eleanor of Aquitaine, was linked to many of these changes.

ACCESS

As you read, use the chart to note the changes that happened in medieval Europe. Each Effect listed tells what happened. Fill in the Cause column with the reasons for each Effect.

CAUSE AND EFFECT

CAUSE	EFFECT
	Eleanor of Aquitaine was queen of France and then became queen of England.
	Nobles had new rules for behavior, and new kinds of literature became popular.
	Gothic architecture replaced Romanesque architecture.
	Life in castles was both safe and comfortable.
	The children of nobles were trained for their roles as adults.

CAST OF CHARACTERS

On the lines provided below, explain why each character was important.

Eleanor of Aquitaine (ah-KWI-tane) _____

Louis VII _____

Henry II _____

Peter Abelard (AB-uh-lard) _____

Hélöise (EL-oh-weez) _____

WORD BANK

annul cosmopolitan tournament mock architecture masonry fortifications

Choose words from the Word Bank to complete the sentences. One word is not used at all.

1. The heavy _____ of Romanesque buildings was not necessary in Gothic structures.

2. Eleanor of Aquitaine was raised in a _____ and cultured home.

3. _____ such as castles protected the people who lived in them from attack.

4. In a _____ knights performed _____ battles to show their skills to crowds of people.

5. When Louis VII wanted to end his marriage, he asked the church to _____ it.

WORD PLAY

Look up the word that you did not use in the dictionary. Write a sentence using that word.

_____

CRITICAL THINKING
MAKING GENERALIZATIONS

A **generalization** is a broad, or general, statement. Readers can find facts or evidence to support and prove that a generalization is valid, or true, in most cases. Read the following generalizations:

A. All seventh graders are taller than sixth graders.

B. Most seventh graders are taller than sixth graders.

C. Every seventh grader is taller than every sixth grader.

Which generalization is valid? You probably know some sixth graders who are taller than some of your seventh grade classmates, so the valid generalization is Sentence B.

Read each generalization below, and look for evidence to support it in Chapter 7, then decide if each generalization is valid.

	Supporting Evidence	Is it valid?
Eleanor of Aquitaine was a well-educated woman.		
Everyone in medieval times enjoyed lyrical poems.		
Gothic cathedrals were more complex buildings than Romanesque churches.		
If a castle had supplies and a source of water, it could outlast a siege.		

WORKING WITH PRIMARY SOURCES

Study the primary source images shown throughout Chapter 7, and read the caption that accompanies each image. Think about the ways that the images reflect what you have read about life in medieval Europe. Then answer the following questions on the lines provided.

1. In what way do the children shown in the image on page 98 reflect a change in lifestyle in medieval Europe?

   _____

2. Look at the image shown on page 100. For what reason might the woman's lover have had to come to her or leave her through a window? Is the image likely to show a real event or a fantasy?

   _____

3. How does the image of the shield on page 101 reflect the idea of courtly love?

   _____

4. Look at the positions of the people watching the jousting match in the image shown on page 103. What generalizations can you make about where viewers are seated and why they are seated there?

   _____

5. Why might a tradesman such as the furrier shown on page 106 be shown in the stained glass window of a church?

   _____

6. What features of the castle shown on page 108 would help to defend the castle from attack?

   _____

7. The author says that Eleanor of Aquitaine's "bold behavior caused a scandal" when she dressed as a warrior to ride to Crusades with Louis VII. In your history journal, write an editorial about Eleanor's actions as if you were a citizen of the time. Explain how Eleanor's actions contrast with the era's expectations for noble women.

WRITE ABOUT IT

Many people believe that the media and popular culture deeply affect the way we behave. Do you agree? How do television, movies, music, newspapers, and magazines affect? Do they have the power to change us or cause us to act differently in some way? Or, do you believe that popular culture simply reflects what already exists? Write a short persuasive essay to answer these questions in your history journal. Provide at least two examples to support your argument.

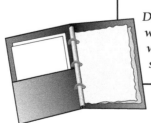

HISTORY JOURNAL

Don't forget to share your history journal with your classmates, and ask if you can see what their journals look like. You might be surprised—and get some new ideas.

ALL OVER THE MAP

Directions: Eleanor of Aquitaine was a key figure in the history of both France and England. Follow the directions for labeling the map to show some of the important places in her life. You may use the map on pages 12–13 as a guide.

- Scan pages 96–98 for the following places.
- Explain why each place was important in Eleanor's life.
- Label the map with the number of each item to show each place's location. Then explain why each place was significant.

1. Aquitaine _____

_____

2. France _____

_____

3. Paris _____

_____

4. Poitiers _____

_____

5. Anjou _____

_____

6. Normandy _____

_____

7. England _____

_____

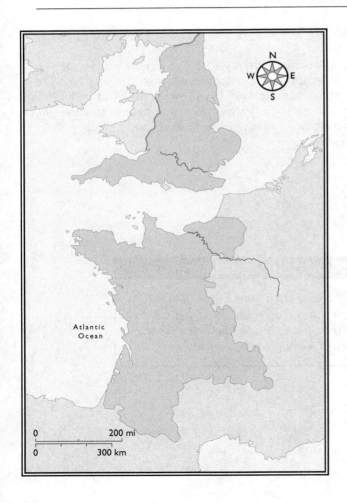

RULERS AND REBELS: ROYAL AUTHORITY AND AMBITION IN ENGLAND, FRANCE, AND GERMANY

CHAPTER SUMMARY

The 12th and 13th centuries in Europe saw times of great ambition, great conflict, and great change. During this time, England's judicial system began to take shape, as did its future government as a constitutional monarchy. Religion continued to be a source of guidance and conflict. Struggles for power between leaders caused borders within Europe to change rapidly.

ACCESS

As you read Chapter 8, review the main ideas about historical events. Then add details to the outline below that provide further information about the main idea's importance.

OUTLINE

MAIN IDEA: Henry II organized a judicial system to help England function smoothly in his absence.

DETAIL: _____

DETAIL: _____

DETAIL: _____

MAIN IDEA: King John was forced to sign the Magna Carta, which set limits on royal powers.

DETAIL: _____

DETAIL: _____

DETAIL: _____

MAIN IDEA: During the reign of Henry III, representatives for nobles and townspeople met in meetings that became known as parliament.

DETAIL: _____

DETAIL: _____

DETAIL: _____

CAST OF CHARACTERS

On the lines provided below, explain why each character was important.

Henry II _____

Thomas à Becket (Tom-us a-BEK-ut) _____

Philip II Augustus (aw-GUS-tus) _____

Frederick I Barbarossa (BAR-buh-row-suh) _____

Richard the Lion-Hearted _____

John I _____

Stephen Langton (LANG-ton) _____

WORD BANK

verdict   charter   allegiance   revenue   judicial   policies   provisions

Choose words from the Word Bank to complete the sentences. One word is not used at all.

1. The system of circuit justices also brought _____ into Henry II's treasury.

2. The _____ signed by King John stated that he could not impose new taxes without the consent of the kingdom.

3. Judges used the _____ of the jury to help them settle disputes over land claims.

4. The Magna Carta included _____ that limited the powers of the king.

5. Henry II's courtiers murdered the archbishop of Canterbury to show _____ to their king.

6. France followed England's example and set up institutions that would help support the _____ of the king.

WORD PLAY

Write a sentence about one of the people from the Cast of Characters for this chapter that uses the word left over from the Word Bank.

_____

_____

WITH A PARENT OR PARTNER

Research the nature of congressional debates in the United States. If you can, watch some of these discussions live on television by tuning into C-Span or another news channel that airs congressional hearings. Then research the nature of the English Parliament's debates and hearings by conducting research in a local library or on the Internet. You may also watch C-Span coverage of the British House of Commons to see these lively debates being enacted. After you have finished your research, compare and contrast the American and British proceedings by filling in a Venn Diagram, noting the differences and similarities. See page 9 in this study guide for a model Venn Diagram. Orally present your completed Venn Diagram to the class.

CRITICAL THINKING
SEQUENCE

Remembering the sequence of related historical events can help you understand larger ideas. Sometimes writers use signal words such as *first, next, then,* and *last* to help show sequence.

Review what you have learned about Richard the Lion-Hearted and the Third Crusade. Complete the sequence chart about him that follows. Use signal words where they make sense.

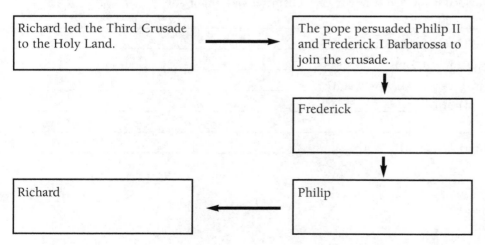

WORKING WITH PRIMARY SOURCES

Examine the illustration of the coronation of John I from Student Edition page 119. In the illustration, one archbishop pours holy oil on John I, while another places the crown on his head. Kings claimed that this ceremony gave them sacred powers that allowed them to overrule the church. The church disagreed.

DRAWING CONCLUSIONS

The illustration shows two archbishops performing holy ceremonies to crown King John. The caption tells how the ceremonies caused a conflict between the church and kings. Think about what conclusions you can draw from these images.

1. What conclusion can you draw about the necessity of the ceremonies?

   _____

   _____

   _____

2. Why do you think that kings felt that their powers allowed them to overrule the church?

   _____

   _____

   _____

3. Why do you think that the church believed that it could not be overruled?

   _____

   _____

   _____

4. Think about what you know about other conflicts between kings and church leaders during the Middle Ages. What conclusion can you draw about these types of conflicts during this time?

   _____

   _____

   _____

WRITE ABOUT IT

The conflict between "church and state" is still apparent in modern times. Think about current sources of tension between American political leaders and religious organizations (e.g., stem cell research, abortion rights, prayer in school, etc.). Choose one controversial topic that pits government leaders against religious leaders and research the two opposing opinions regarding the issue. Then write a persuasive essay in your history journal that states your opinion in regard to the issue and research to support that opinion.

ALL OVER THE MAP

Directions Follow the steps listed below to complete the map.

- Review Chapter 8 to revisit events in and around the Angevin Empire during the 12th and 13th centuries.
- Label the following cities: London, Paris, Canterbury, Runnymede.
- Choose colors to identify the following people: Philip II, Frederick I Barbarossa, Thomas à Becket, and King John I. Add to the legend to explain who each color stands for.
- Use Philip II's color to draw a circle around the land he took away from King John.
- Use Frederick's color to draw a circle around the land he acquired through marriage.
- Use Thomas à Becket's color to draw an arrow from the place he had resided to where he was sent in exile by Henry II.
- Use King John's color to circle where he was forced to sign the Magna Carta in 1215.

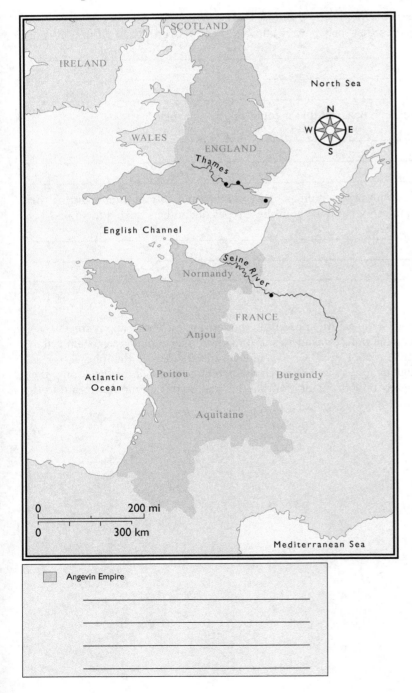

Legend:
Angevin Empire

EMPIRE ON EARTH, KINGDOM OF HEAVEN: POLITICS, POPES, AND RELIGIOUS CONFLICTS

CHAPTER SUMMARY

Like other European rulers, German emperor Frederick II came into conflict with the papacy. At the same time, the Catholic church was dealing with religious problems within the church. As people began to question basic beliefs, the church approved the founding of new orders of monks to preach their faith.

ACCESS

The Catholic church had conflicts with European leaders, and within the church itself. As you read Chapter 9, make a main idea map (see page 8 of this study guide) to organize the details that support the main idea at the center of the map.

MAIN IDEA: The Catholic church had conflicts with European rulers, and with people questioning its beliefs.

DETAIL: Conflicts with Frederick II

DETAIL: Conflicts with Peter of Aragon

DETAIL: Conflicts with heretics

DETAIL: Preaching to heretics

CAST OF CHARACTERS

Write a sentence about why each character was important.

Frederick II _____

Pope Innocent III (IN-uh-sent) _____

Peter of Aragon _____

Dominic (DOM-uh-nik) _____

Francis of Assisi (uh-SEE-zee) _____

WHAT HAPPENED WHEN

Write the events that happened on these dates.

1198 _____

1215 _____

1250 _____

1282 _____

Use the timeline graphic organizer to make a Chapter 9 timeline. Include the dates above, and do some research to add dates for events such as the founding of the Dominican order, the founding of the Franciscan order, and the dates of Frederick's crusade.

WORD BANK

diplomacy excommunicate ordeal heretics humility mendicant

Choose words from the Word Bank to complete the sentences. One word is not used at all.

1. Dominican and Franciscan monks lived lives of _____ and virtue.

2. The church called the Albigensians _____.

3. Frederick's use of _____ to accomplish the goal of his crusade avoided warfare.

4. _____ orders of monks begged for food and money.

5. The pope decided to _____ Frederick after he refused to go on a crusade.

WORD PLAY

Look up the word that you did not use in the dictionary. Write a sentence using that word in a contemporary context.

_____

WITH A PARENT OR PARTNER

Find an example, recent or historical, of a leader who tried to use diplomacy to solve problems or conflicts. Make a chart that states *the problem* the leader faced, *how he or she used diplomacy* to try to solve it, and the *outcome* of his or her actions.

CRITICAL THINKING
MAIN IDEA AND DETAILS

A **main idea** is the most important idea in a paragraph or section of text. **Details** are the examples, reasons, and facts that explain or support the main idea.

Reread the first two paragraphs of Chapter 9 on Student Edition page 123. Notice that the details give more information about the main idea.

Main Idea: Three key figures shaped the destiny of Frederick II of Germany.

   Detail: He inherited rule of Sicily from one of his grandfathers.

   Detail: He inherited rule of Germany from his other grandfather.

   Detail: His guardian was Pope Innocent III.

Write details from the chapter that support each of the main ideas below.

1. Main Idea: Frederick was comfortable with people of the Arabic, Byzantine, and Latin cultures.

   Detail: _____

   Detail: _____

2. Main Idea: Frederick was curious about the natural world.

   Detail: _____

   Detail: _____

3. Main Idea: The pope created a problem when he decided that the French should rule Sicily.

   Detail: _____

   Detail: _____

WORKING WITH PRIMARY SOURCES

Francis of Assisi gave his followers this rule. Read his rule, and then answer the questions that follow.

The Official Rule of the Franciscans

The brothers shall appropriate nothing to themselves, neither a house, nor a place . . . they shall confidently go seeking for alms. Nor need they be ashamed, for the Lord made Himself poor for us in this world. [Poverty] has made you poor in possessions, [but] has exalted you in virtues.

MAKING INFERENCES

1. Francis says that his followers should keep nothing for themselves. Who do you think he wants things such as a house to go to?

   _____

   _____

2. The rule tells brothers to "confidently go seeking for alms." Why would being confident be important to follow this rule? If necessary, use a dictionary to check the meaning of *alms*.

   _____

   _____

3. The rules tell the brothers not to be ashamed of their poverty. Why might Francis have thought that the brothers would be ashamed?

   _____

   _____

4. Francis made a point of telling his followers to live in poverty. What inference can you make about how priests and other monks lived at the time?

   _____

   _____

5. Francis tells his followers that poverty "has exalted you in virtues." What virtues might his followers have gained from their poverty?

   _____

   _____

WRITE ABOUT IT

What rule do you follow that you think would help others to live a good life? Write an essay for your history journal in which you state your rule and explain why you think it is important to follow.

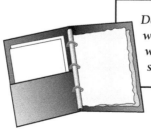

HISTORY JOURNAL

Don't forget to share your history journal with your classmates, and ask if you can see what their journals look like. You might be surprised—and get some new ideas.

ALL OVER THE MAP

Directions Relative Location can be described by explaining the distance or direction from one place to another. Use the compass rose on map below to explain the relative locations of the places that follow. For example:

Where are the Alps in relation to Paris?

The Alps are southeast of Paris.

1. Where is Paris in relation to Cologne? _____

2. Where is Albi in relation to Avignon? _____

3. Where is Bologna in relation to Venice? _____

4. Where is Assisi in relation to Rome? _____

5. Where is Rome in relation to Naples? _____

6. Where is Aragon in relation to the Kingdom of Sicily? _____

7. Where is London in relation to Rome? _____

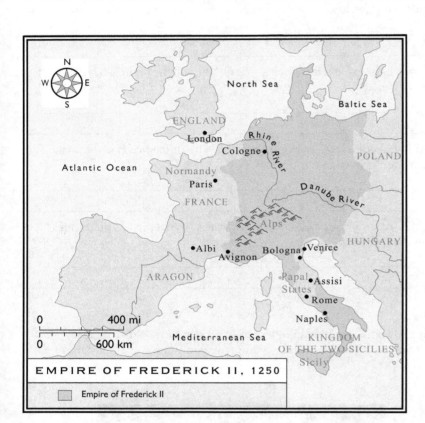

EMPIRE OF FREDERICK II, 1250

▢ Empire of Frederick II

HIGH IDEALS AND LOW MANEUVERS: THE RISE OF UNIVERSITIES AND THE DECLINE OF THE PAPACY

CHAPTER SUMMARY

During the 13th century, young men could attend student-run schools or universities run by masters. Some women learned how to read, but they could not go to universities. The leading intellectual was a scholar named Thomas Aquinas. He wrote how to organize a society for the good of all. During this time, conflicts over power broke out between European monarchs and the papacy.

ACCESS

Chapter 10 describes how universities developed, the intellectual legacy of Thomas Aquinas, and conflicts between monarchs and the papacy. To organize the information in the chapter, use the chart below. As you read the chapter, look for details to add in each category. Record them in the correct column.

Schools and Universities	Thomas Aquinas	Politics and the Papacy

CAST OF CHARACTERS

Write a short paragraph for each pair of historical figures to describe the nature of their relationship with one another.

Thomas Aquinas (uh-KWAI-nus) and the Dominicans (dow-MIN-uh-kuns) _____

_____

_____

King Philip IV (FIL-up) and Pope Boniface VIII (BON-uh-fus) _____

_____

_____

WORD BANK

Use each pair of vocabulary words in a sentence about the chapter.

1. **patron, theology** _____

2. **guild, university** _____

3. **philosophy, natural law** _____

WORD PLAY

Look up the word *persecution* in the dictionary. Write an original sentence using the word.

_____

WITH A PARENT OR PARTNER

With a parent or a partner, brainstorm ways in which Thomas Aquinas's ideas about good government apply to your community. List ways that the local, state, or federal government works for the good of your town or city. Think of ways in which citizens work for the good of others, too. After you have completed this list, create a separate list of ways in which government worked for the good of the people during Aquinas's time.

CRITICAL THINKING
MAKING COMPARISONS AND CONTRASTS

When you make a **comparison**, you look for how two things are alike. Words that signal comparisons include *similar, both,* and *the same as.* To show a **contrast**, you look for how two things are different. Words that signal contrasts include *however, on the other hand,* and *but.* Discuss this example with a partner: What is being compared? What differences are mentioned?

COMPARISON	CONTRAST
Both the Tartar society and the European society had roles for men and women.	The Tartars were nomadic people, but most people in Europe lived in towns or cities.

Compare and contrast Aristotle's philosophy of logic with Thomas Aquinas's interpretation. Write differences and similarities in the Venn diagram below. Discuss your answers with a partner.

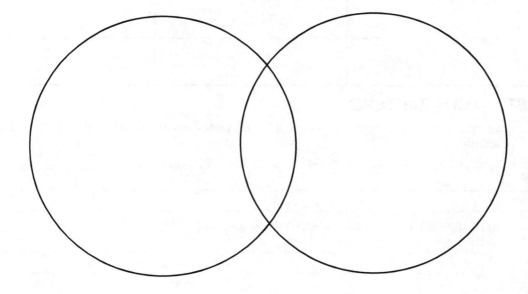

WORKING WITH PRIMARY SOURCES

Study the illustrations from a medieval medical textbook on Student Edition page 143, and read the caption. Discuss with a partner how learning medicine at the school in Salerno, Sicily, prepared students for surgery and other medical practices shown in the pictures. Share your thoughts with the class.

DRAWING CONCLUSIONS

As books became more easily produced in the 13th century, more medical texts were written. They dealt with such topics as how to mix medicines and how to conduct surgery. Use this information and what you already know to help you answer the questions.

1. What types of treatments are shown on Student Edition page 143?

_____

_____

2. How might this page be helpful to a person practicing medicine in the 13th century?

_____

_____

3. How is this page an example of the limits of medical knowledge?

_____

_____

4. Why might doctors want to purchase a book instead of relying on their experience?

_____

_____

WRITE ABOUT IT

According to the textbook, the most prestigious university degree in 13th-century Europe was a degree in theology. What degrees do you think most Americans currently consider as "prestigious"? Write an essay in your history journal explaining whether or not these degrees deserve their reputation as prestigious.

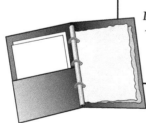

HISTORY JOURNAL

Don't forget to share your history journal with your classmates, and ask if you can see what their journals look like. You might be surprised—and get some new ideas.

GROUP TOGETHER

Wouldn't it be fun to know what other students think about education in medieval Europe? How does it compare to schooling today? Get a few friends together and ask your teacher to help you organize a discussion group at school. Have one person take notes and another person present the group's ideas to the class.

ALL OVER THE MAP

Directions Follow the directions below to complete the map.

- Scan pages 136–142 in the Student Edition to find information on some of the universities shown on the map.

- Add an icon or a symbol for areas of study offered at different universities.

- Draw each icon or symbol on the map.

- Make a legend for your map showing what each icon stands for.

- Give your map a title that explains what the map shows.

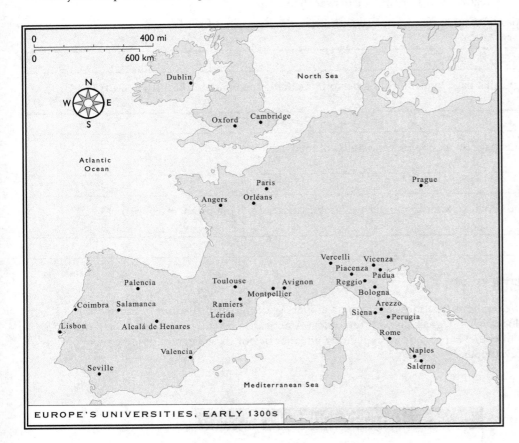

MATTERS OF LIFE AND DEATH: FAMINE, PLAGUE, AND WAR

CHAPTER SUMMARY

Widespread famine and the bubonic plague reduced Europe's population by more than a third in the early 14th century. New social structures began to emerge as merchants and craftsmen formed guilds and set up apprenticeship systems. Town governments reflected the growing power of the working people.

ACCESS

Chapter 11 discusses how famine and plague had widespread consequences for Europe. As you read about the famine, note the effects of each cause on the chart below. Use the cause and effect chart on page 9 in this study guide to create a similar chart that identifies the causes and effects of the plague.

CAUSE	EFFECT
Europe's population increases steadily.	
Soils are overused and/or infertile.	
Climate changes result in too much rain.	
Food becomes even more scarce.	
Starving people commit desperate acts.	

CAST OF CHARACTERS

On the lines provided below, write a sentence about why each character was important.

Giovanni Boccaccio (jee-oh-VAN-ee bo-KOCH-chee-oh) _____

Ibn Khaldun (ib-UN Kal-DOON) _____

Philip IV (FIL-up) _____

Edward III _____

Richard II _____

WORD BANK

consumers pneumonia famine prejudice bylaws standards infant mortality

Choose words from the Word Bank to complete the sentences. One word is not used at all.

1. One form of the plague was very much like _____.

2. The apprenticeship system helped _____ feel confident about goods they purchased.

3. Town governments developed _____ to help create order in their villages.

4. _____ caused some Christians to think that Jews were responsible for the plague.

5. Starvation led to higher rates of _____ among the poor.

6. Poor harvests due to climate changes contributed to a widespread _____.

WORD PLAY

Write a sentence about the guild system that uses the word left over in the Word Bank.

_____

_____

WITH A PARENT OR PARTNER

In what ways do consumers have power today? Ask a parent or partner about how he or she makes choices as a consumer. Discuss how the consumers' choices affect which goods and services are made available. Make a list of ways that consumers can exercise their power and voice their concerns or needs.

CRITICAL THINKING
MAKING PREDICTIONS

Making predictions as you read can help you link historical events. As you read, use what you already know along with new information to help you make predictions.

Review what you have learned about the plague. Use the chart to describe new information you have learned about peasants in England. Then make predictions about what social and governmental changes may occur.

What I Know	What I Learned	Predictions
The huge numbers of deaths resulting from the plague greatly reduced Europe's population.	Peasants began to realize that their work was _____ _____ _____. They revolted when kings and nobles _____ _____ _____.	The serf system will probably _____ _____ Support for the monarchy will probably _____ _____. Local government will probably _____ _____

WORKING WITH PRIMARY SOURCES

This passage, which appears in a sidebar on Student Edition page 158, is from a chronicle by an English monk. It describes how peasants were influenced to revolt in 1381.

> The [peasants] had as their counselor a chaplain of evil disposition named Sir John Ball, who advised them to get rid of all the lords and of archbishops and bishops . . . saying that their possessions should be distributed among the laity.

MAKING INFERENCES

1. What can you infer about the monk's opinion of Sir John Ball? What evidence from the quotation supports your idea?

   _____

   _____

2. What can you tell about Ball's opinion of nobles and religious leaders? What evidence from the quotation supports your idea?

   _____

   _____

3. What can you infer from the quotation about the stability of the power structure in late 14th-century England?

   _____

   _____

WRITE ABOUT IT

What do you think about how power and wealth are distributed in our society? Write an essay in your history journal about a way that you would like to change or improve our society's structure. Explain how this could be accomplished.

ALL OVER THE MAP

Directions Follow the steps below to complete the map.

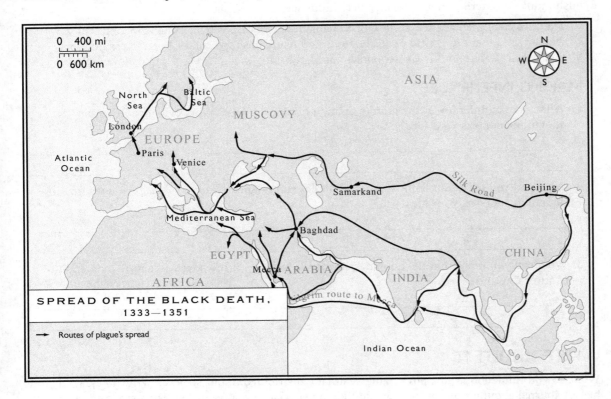

SPREAD OF THE BLACK DEATH, 1333—1351

→ Routes of plague's spread

- Review Student Edition pages 148–155 to find information on famines and the plague.
- Check the map on Student Edition pages 14–15 or an atlas to identify country or city names not shown on the map.
- Choose a color to indicate European countries that farmed infertile soils by the late 13th century and color these areas on the map. Add this color and its meaning to the map legend.
- Choose a different color to indicate which area was most affected by climate changes early in the 14th century and color this area on the map. Add this color and its meaning to the map legend.
- Locate the city that Giovanni Boccaccio wrote about in *The Decameron*. Create an icon for this city, such as a B with a circle around it, and add it to the map. Add the icon and its meaning to the map legend.
- Locate two European cities that lost half their populations to the plague. Create an icon for them and draw them next to the cities on the map. Add the icon and its meaning to the map legend.

THE END OF THE OLD AND THE BEGINNING OF THE NEW: THE MIDDLE AGES GIVES WAY TO THE RENAISSANCE

CHAPTER SUMMARY

During the late Middle Ages, societies changed through warfare and inventions. In Spain, the king and queen persecuted the Muslim and Jewish populations during the Spanish Inquisition. Conflicts within the Catholic church led to changing beliefs.

ACCESS

Chapter 12 describes the effects of warfare and persecution in Europe, conflicts with the church, and inventions that changed how ordinary people lived. To organize the information, use the sequence graphic organizer on page 9 in this study guide. As you read each section, record the order of events. Remember that the events may not be written in the correct sequence.

Joan of Arc to the Rescue

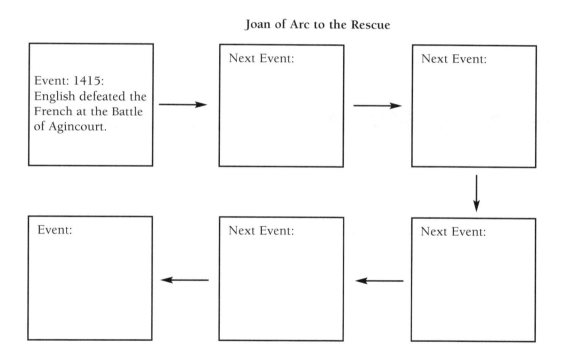

Event: 1415: English defeated the French at the Battle of Agincourt. → Next Event: → Next Event:

↓

Event: ← Next Event: ← Next Event:

CAST OF CHARACTERS

For each pair of historic figures, write a paragraph that describes their relationship and how that relationship influenced the course of history.

Charles VII and Joan of Arc (ARK) _____

_____

_____

Isabella (is-uh-BEL-uh) and Ferdinand (FUR-di-nand) _____

_____

_____

WORD BANK

raw materials   heresy   monarchy   parliament   inquisitions   salvation

Choose words from the Word Bank to complete the sentences. Two words are not used at all.

1. Joan of Arc was accused of _____ and burned at the stake.

2. Cloth manufacturers needed access to _____ to make their goods.

3. Christians went on pilgrimages to try to gain _____.

4. King Ferdinand and Queen Isabella held religious trials called _____.

WORD PLAY

Look up in a dictionary the two words that you did not use. Write a sentence using both words.

_____

WITH A PARENT OR PARTNER

You read that England's foe was France. A synonym of *foe* is *enemy*. With a parent or partner, find a synonym for the following words that relate to the Hundred Years War: *disputes, chronicle, pillage,* and *bravery*. Use a dictionary or a thesaurus if you need extra help. Then write a paragraph in your history journal using some of these words to discuss an aspect of the Hundred Years War.

CRITICAL THINKING
DISTINGUISH BETWEEN FACT AND OPINION

Remember that a **fact** is a statement that can be proven true. An **opinion** is a statement of someone's belief. Look at this example from page 161. Where might you check the fact for accuracy? What evidence supports the opinion?

FACT	OPINION
Edward plunged England and France into the Hundred Years' War.	Edward III of England was, in many ways, the ideal medieval king.

Read each statement about events or people from the chapter. Label each statement as a fact or as an opinion. For each opinion, underline the clues.

1. During the Battle at Crécy, Edward had the better position, a hilltop. _____

2. The longbow was accurate and was easily reloaded. _____

3. Foot soldiers came from both the peasantry and the lower ranks of townsmen.

_____

4. One of the most notable Yorkists to hold the throne was King Richard III.

_____

5. Richard III was accused of having his nephews murdered. _____

6. Isabella and Ferdinand sponsored the voyages of Christopher Columbus.

_____

WORKING WITH PRIMARY SOURCES

Read the sidebar from Student Edition page 168. It was written by Gomes Eannes de Azura, the chief archivist and royal chronicler of the kingdom of Portugal.

> [Henry the Navigator] always kept ships well armed against the Infidel, both for war, and because he had also a wish to know the land that lay beyond the isles of Canary and Cape Bojador [Morocco].

IDENTIFYING POINT OF VIEW

Henry the Navigator was the prince of Portugal. Throughout his life he supported exploration and the study of navigation. He sponsored between 30 and 40 voyages along the western African coast.

1. Why might the author of the quotation show a bias?

_____

_____

2. Who might the *Infidel* be? Check a dictionary if you are not sure.

_____

_____

3. What new information do you learn about Henry the Navigator?

_____

_____

4. What sources might you use to verify the facts in the quotation?

_____

_____

WRITE ABOUT IT

Though most parts of the world have been thoroughly explored by the 21st century, there are other kinds of exploration still to be done (e.g., genetics research, space exploration, environmental studies, etc.). Think about an area of exploration that needs more attention or funding. Write an essay in your history journal to explain why you think exploration in this area is necessary.

ALL OVER THE MAP

Directions Follow the steps below to complete the map.

- Scan pages 161–166 to find information on the Hundred Years' War.
- Add arrows of different colors to show the paths of armies. Add the arrows and their colors to the map legend.
- Add dates that correspond to battles.
- Share your map with a partner to show your changes.

THE HUNDRED YEARS' WAR,
1345—1453

English victory   French victory

English control at its largest extent, 1429

_____

_____

NAME

LIBRARY / MEDIA CENTER RESEARCH LOG

DUE DATE

Brainstorm: Other Sources and Places to Look

Places I **Know** to Look

What I Need to **Find**

I need to use:

☐ primary sources.
☐ secondary

WHAT I FOUND

Title/Author/Location (call # or URL)

How I Found it

- Web link
- Internet Search
- Browsing
- Library Catalog
- Suggestion

- Secondary Source
- Primary Source

- Other
- Website
- Book/Periodical

Rate each source from 1 (low) to 4 (high) in the categories below

helpful   relevant

CPSIA information can be obtained
at www.ICGtesting.com
Printed in the USA
BVHW011035160419
545663BV00001B/4/P